Watching Momma Die

Watching Momma Die

Carol M. Gilligan

iUniverse, Inc.
New York Lincoln Shanghai

Watching Momma Die

All Rights Reserved © 2004 by Carol M. Gilligan

No part of this book may be reproduced or transmitted in any form or by any means, graphic, electronic, or mechanical, including photocopying, recording, taping, or by any information storage retrieval system, without the written permission of the publisher.

iUniverse, Inc.

For information address:
iUniverse, Inc.
2021 Pine Lake Road, Suite 100
Lincoln, NE 68512
www.iuniverse.com

ISBN: 0-595-32615-3

Printed in the United States of America

Watching Momma Die

Carol M. Gilligan

iUniverse, Inc.
New York Lincoln Shanghai

Watching Momma Die

All Rights Reserved © 2004 by Carol M. Gilligan

No part of this book may be reproduced or transmitted in any form or by any means, graphic, electronic, or mechanical, including photocopying, recording, taping, or by any information storage retrieval system, without the written permission of the publisher.

iUniverse, Inc.

For information address:
iUniverse, Inc.
2021 Pine Lake Road, Suite 100
Lincoln, NE 68512
www.iuniverse.com

ISBN: 0-595-32615-3

Printed in the United States of America

This book is dedicated to Momma,
Adele R. Gilligan

She gave to me more than I will ever be able to repay.

Yesterday, today, forever.

I love you!

ACKNOWLEDGMENTS

It is difficult to remember everyone who gave of themselves, their time, their love and help during the months leading up to Momma's death. I do not intend to purposely omit anyone, for I believe all who were there for Momma and the family are special people. My thanks go out to everyone who knew and cared for Momma during her illness and who leant support to me during and after her death, you know who you are.

My heartfelt thanks especially go to a handful of close friends. Without them I would never have been able to cope with it all.

Regina Chase, you are indeed a friend above friends. Maureen Hillery, your support and care, not only of me but toward Momma will never be forgotten. For Jennifer Lynch and Chris Bills, because you helped me to laugh when I needed it most. To Julia Morgan, Momma's 'guardian angel". but my greatest thanks must go to God, for without Her inspiration and urging I would never have accomplished this writing. Again, thank-you one and all for your love and patience.

I still had hope when I walked into the hospital room. I still had hope, even though Momma was lying there unable to respond to me. I hoped, as I watched the nurses coming and going, doing for Momma what she could no longer do for herself. I hoped, when I finally was able to speak to the doctor and he told me it was only a matter of time now before she would need assisted living, she wasn't going to get better.

Momma was released that day and I took her home, all the while I still hoped. I knew in my heart that she should still be in the care of professionals. Professionals, who were able to give Momma the care she needed, the care I couldn't, but there was no choice. She couldn't stay in the hospital any longer she had to go home. It was almost impossible to deal with. Three days later, when her condition worsened, Dad and I had to make a decision about finding a nursing home for Momma. Those days were hell. The calling and meeting with people who are so busy, just talking to them is a near miracle. Then you must wait for the answers, all the while you continue to try to be optimistic and hopeful.

I watched the woman who used to do all the necessary things I needed no longer able to do the simplest tasks on her own. It was heartrending and there is nothing you can do to alter that for her. Suddenly, you are her world, her only world. Not that others cease to exist but because her life, her new home, her new routine are placed in your hands. Everything changes. I did not want that responsibility but neither did anyone else. My father was so confused and defeated by the ordeal that he was at a loss. My two brothers showed up only to save face at the last minute. Warm bodies fulfilling an obligation. The one brother was too *busy* and wouldn't take time off work but was quick to express his gratitude in my being there to take care of *things*. The other brother and eldest not playing any part at all. Both watched from a distance, indifferent. That left me.

I live a thousand miles from my parents. I too have a job, a home, as well as a life. We also shared one Mother. We will never have another one; it is the common thread in all people. Still I was expected to do the right thing, have all the right answers, know all the right moves to make, like a good sister and daughter should. I was left to make all the decisions. I wanted nothing more than to "kidnap" Momma, bring her to live with me, where she would be safe. We could pick up right where we left off, before the hospital, before the doctor, before the responsibility. Far away from the pills and bedpans and those "dignified" adult diapers Momma depended on now. I wanted to make it all better so neither she nor I would have to deal with the reality of what was happening to us both now. Not to have to contend with all the things a child has to when the tables are turned and a parent is in need.

I thought I had prepared myself long ago for the **big issue**. Prepared myself mentally and emotionally for the inevitable. I knew someday this would need to be addressed as real, as a fact of life. So did my brothers. But it is different when the time comes. Everyone wants to avoid the topic and pretend it doesn't exist or things will get better and all can go back to the way things were. I had asked questions of my parents, made suggestions many times, stepping back to allow them to work through the "hush-hush" business that goes with final preparations. I knew though, down deep inside, when it came right down to it, I would have to be the one with the guts necessary to say, "It's okay Momma, you don't have to fight this monster any longer." Nobody wants to face that. Nobody wants to say those things; I didn't want to…but I did. It took me at least a week to rehearse how I would say those words and when I felt it the right time, I said them. No one else in the family wanted that responsibility either; no one else had the guts or the love it took to say those words or grant the permission many dying people need to die in peace. They conveniently went back to work, back to the safety of their homes, back watching from a distance to avoid getting their hands dirty while I assumed the role of the bad guy. I was left with that responsibility and I did it. I don't know if I did it good or not, but I did it.

My one brother is a nurse. He works in a geriatric hospital. He works with the aged, the dying and the hopeless everyday. My Father said he thought that because my brother works in that field everyday he did not want to be there with Momma. I think that's a pretty poor excuse. I believe it was a choice he made. He had all the answers though, the signs, the next step as the disease progressed, what to expect, just no time. He managed to give Momma four hours of his time the Saturday before she died, four hours out of his busy schedule. He told everyone he had to get right back to work because he was afraid they would lay him off. This same man was voted Nurse of the year in Wisconsin in 2003. They had a dinner in his honor, he received an award and even the Governor of the state was in attendance to congratulate him. I don't accept his excuse about being laid off. People who are dying no longer need to put on airs. They are open and honest. It does not seem to matter to them what others think. They do not need to hide their feelings they say what they mean. After he left that Saturday, Momma said to me, "I don't know why he even bothered to come." I never mentioned to him what Momma said. It took all I could to convince him to come in the first place. He is still upset with me today about asking him to come see Momma. Five days later, Momma died.

On the night Momma passed away though he called me, leaving a message at the motel where I was staying. He said, "Happy New Year", and then hung up. What kind of a message was that? I did not respond. I didn't need to hear him tell me how devastated he was or how grateful he was to me for my being there with Momma and all the things I had done. I couldn't go there with him. I couldn't play those games; instead I talked with two of my friends. Friends standing by, waiting on news from me. Friends, ready to book flights, to lend support. To lend love. Shoulders to lean on, shoulders broad enough, to be the pillars of strength that I needed right now. Friends who had traveled the thousand miles with me on other occasions to share in the love and person Momma had been. No, I couldn't and won't go there with him. No games, no excuses, no more.

My other brother ran scared from Momma's illness. Ran scared from the illness and impending death, afraid of what it meant. Too afraid of losing, too afraid of truth.

I stood alone watching Momma die. During her final moments of life. She and I drifting alone on a sea of hope.

What ever happened to "Honor thy Father and thy Mother"? Where did that commandment go? Why is giving of self, loving and cherishing others out of fashion? What has happened to us and what does that hold for us? Have we wandered so far from important truths that we no longer value life and tending to the old, the lonely, the dying? What are we running away from but our own mortality?

In the months before Momma died, her health began to diminish at a rapid rate. It wasn't necessarily a surprise that her health was weakening leading to her eventual death but it is always a shock. I came to visit her several times in the past two years during that period. It was obvious that her condition was not good and she became more and more susceptible to whatever was floating around. As she approached the end of her life, she contracted other diseases as a result of complications caused by her deteriorating condition. Diabetes, congestive heart failure, thrush mouth. The list was long and seemed endless. It seemed like Momma had enough wrong with her for several people but she kept her spirits up, waiting for our next visit. She lived for those visits.

Her breathing almost seemed artificial and I wanted desperately to help her with it. The gasping for air, the labor required in doing that one unconscious act, was such an on going battle for her now. I didn't know if she would be able to take another breath but she did, for about two hours.

We talked. Talked about anything I could think of, just so she would know I was there. Talked and hoped but that didn't help, she died despite all my hopes and I watched powerless to do anything about it. I stood watching Momma die in disbelief. The gasping stopped and her life was over.

One of the biggest "pickles" about life is its eventual end. The journey that connects us all. We become pioneers forging into a new wilderness, threading across unknown territory, into an unconquerable and inescapable frontier. Death is not partial. We do not get to pick or choose. Death makes no distinction between rich or poor, race, color or creed. Education, fame and beauty play no part in its selection. Despite all we believe or are taught, when it comes to death, we are all equal. Death is our fate, our destiny and a goal we all eventually attain. At some point in our lives we are witness to or participants in its inevitable persuasion. Death and loss become as much a reality as birth and aging, sneaking into our lives to remind us, it is ultimately in control, fair or not. Through loss, death prompts us to take hold of life, allowing us to grasp hold of how fragile the gift of life really is and how quickly it can be taken away. No second chances.

I was afraid when Momma died. I am 48 years old and as stubborn and independent as Momma had raised me to be. A fighter, a survivor, just like her but I was afraid. Afraid and alone. She was gone. How frail she looked. Her physical life beaten and battered. How I needed her comfort right now. Her color changed so quickly once her heartbeat the last time, she looked like a wax figure instead of the bright blue-eyed lady she always was. At that moment I was aware that the lifeless figure lying there in the hospital bed was no longer my Momma. She had made the final step. She had freed herself from the months of pain, the inability to function in the manner she always had. I continued to talk to her even though they had officially declared her dead at 8:00p.m. It was now 8:22p.m.

Death as a rule is not a hot topic. We do not get together to discuss it over drinks. It is not advertised nor promoted. It is for the most part, taboo in our culture and we live attempting to stay as far away from it as possible until it stares us right in the face. Yet death is very much a part of living and plays a major role, it is our final stage of growth and one which needs to be prepared for and embraced as we journey home.

Death. The idea is frightening. It is frightening because we do not understand it. It is frightening because we do not understand it and we must do it alone. No instructions, no experience, no visible assurance that once we "cross over" anything awaits us. I know these thoughts, I have them.

No matter how many times loss enters our lives we do not get used to it. We do not become hardened to its effects or influence it instills in us. It is always shocking and painful. Grief, sorrow and hurt are afflictions we must endure not only at the time of loss but for weeks, months and even years after. At times memories open the floodgates to the past causing us to re-live the experience over and over again. We are never totally able to block out the result of losing someone or the pain that it imposes in our lives.

I continued to talk with Momma. I talked about things she and I had shared together in our lives as well as things we had done in the last few years. Momma's biggest dream was to go on a cruise, so in 1998, I gave her that wish for Christmas. Just us girls. We spent two memorable weeks together in Florida at Disney World and on a week long Disney Cruise. We went to the Bahamas and Castaway Cay. We had a wonderful time together. She was so happy.

In September of 2002, I made arrangements to come and get Momma and bring her to my home in Colorado for a two-week vacation. How ***alive*** she was to that, what hope that must have given her amid her dawning journey to come. I believe she knew then it was only a matter of time, she knew hanging on with all the hope she had.

Still I talked, on and on and on. I don't recall in those last minutes with Momma who came and went. I just wanted her to know I was still there with her regardless and so, I talked, just like I was there for a visit in the middle of a bright sunny afternoon at her house. I didn't want her to be alone. I wanted Momma to be safe; she was so precious to me. She was so little lying there and so I stood there talking and looking at her but not hoping any more. My hope had just died.

I first met Momma on December 19, 1954, in the wee hours of the night. I don't know if she chose me or if I chose her but we became fast friends. She and I shared much in our brief time together, little things that I recall about her now that once were of little significance, have taken on new meaning and purpose. Today however, those things are filled with thoughts of love and are cherished. Memories of Momma that people share with me today cause me to realize I have forgotten so much that others will never know about her.

I remember a couple weeks before Momma died; she asked me if I thought she would ever feel better. I lied. I said, "Yes." Looking at her laying there on her deathbed now I knew I hadn't lied at all. I knew she felt better.

Death comes in many disguises. Sometimes death comes to us resembling a dark sinister shadow that sweeps down upon its victim stealing them away. At other times death dons the garments of a blessing, gently caressing and embracing us into a new life. At times death can be harsh and hurried and at times death is patient and kind in its selection. But once death comes calling, it never departs unaccompanied.

At first death rapped politely in Momma's life, then as time passed by, death became more and more insistent as it rattled nosily around who Momma was. Despite the locks and bolts barring its entrance, the intruder managed to break and enter.

Momma was not as responsive to anyone in the last week of her life. She seemed to be working through other more important issues, things beyond our reach. I believe Momma knew who was there though; she would suddenly perk up and say she had been visiting with my Aunt Minnie in Waterloo or chatting with her friend Rosy across town and I knew she really had been. She struggled to stay with us even though the pull to leave was getting greater and more demanding. She began to worry more and more about Dad and I think she was able to finally understand when I assured her he would be okay. She smiled and nodded in a way that spoke of child-like innocence and trust.

I wanted nothing more than to run away. I didn't want to be a part of any of this. I didn't want to see Momma like this. They tell us one of the steps in the dying process is denial, followed eventually by acceptance. I think both the dying person and those close to them experience the process together. I wanted to deny what I knew, what I watched happening to Momma. I prayed as two separate people, one still clinging to hope and the other praying for an end to the suffering Momma was enduring. I believe in many ways those prayers were selfish, I do not know if I was praying totally for Momma or the pain it was causing me.

When death strikes, it leaves you with a sick nauseating feeling somewhere in the depths of your being. A hollow emptiness that washes over your person long after the actual death. It leaves absolute sorrow and sadness in its wake without pity. One feels abandoned, betrayed and cheated. Alone to your own grief and in my own loss I knew I was thinking only of myself. Despite the lingering illness Momma experienced, I wanted more time with her. Death had stolen her from me before "*I*" was ready. I wanted so badly to sit one more time upon the swing out back, plant one more flower, sing one more song with Momma as we watched the sun set on one more day together. I wanted one more moment to let the cool breeze blow through our lives. I wanted this for me. I wanted this regardless of the fact that I knew how sick she was.

During one of the last days before Momma died, while I was visiting with her, she woke and told me, "They were calling her on the phone, trying to get a hold of her." I understood, even if she couldn't tell me who the "they" were. I understood only too well and I got nervous. The following day Momma was visibly irritated by something and stated; "I am in an awful position here." She groped and grasped at invisible things. She shifted and moved from side to side continually as if preparing to get up and leave. The struggle to stay versus the compelling and urgent need to go was tremendous and now was consuming her every minute. I watched Momma die in bits and pieces for two months and then as the bits and pieces gave way to larger and larger chunks. The grieving process began not when Momma died but about three months prior to the actual death. It is a course of action that cannot be hurried. It is a journey that takes place little by little, step by step each day until you finally accept the loss as real. The letting go is a healing that deserves time. It is necessary and vital, requiring a strength not immediately available but one, which in it's own time arrives.

Dad called on Thanksgiving to say Momma wasn't doing very well. He had to take her to the hospital, she was sick again. You could hear it is his voice, the fear, the reality, and his need. I flew back home. I was scared when I walked into her room at the hospital, unsure about what was happening. Momma brightened a bit when I came in and said she felt better just knowing I was there. She looked like hell. She had thinned and her face told of how much she had been through in the last while.

We had quite a relationship, Momma and I. Rocky at times but because of those moments in our lives, it made us stronger. We grew to respect each other and as a result, we became best of friends. Momma and I were on the same wavelength, even exchanging similar gifts at holidays. There was a link, a bond, that not even time or distance could sever and we were proud of each other, proud of who we were.

I stayed for two weeks, watching the monster inside Momma kill her a little more each day. We arranged for Mercy Home Care the day she left the hospital while starting plans to find a nursing home. We didn't have any choice about nursing homes, if you don't have the available funding you basically go wherever there is an empty bed. You "settle" for whatever you can get. You worry the whole while and hope she will get the care she needs. The horror stories one hears about nursing homes makes you nervous and anxious. There is nothing left for you to do but hope. Hope that it will be okay, hope that you made the right decisions, hope that they will be kind to her. Hope, hope, hope.

Momma was released from Mercy Medical Center on Friday. It was determined she couldn't remain there any longer, insurance reasons and such. Her condition was poor. She was totally unable to walk, unable to feed herself, unable to dress or undress. She could not go to the bathroom unassisted or take the multitude of pills she required on her own. She needed 24 hour care, 7 days a week. It was Friday. It was 5:30p.m. What the hell was I supposed to do? I didn't have a clue. That was the morning her physician, Dr. Schmid, took me aside and told me Momma was not going to get better. He said it was time we thought about placing her in a nursing facility. Her heart was wearing out and it was only a matter of time. He told me so I could tell my Father. He told me so I could tell my brothers. He told me so someone would pick up the responsibility no one else wanted. It was only a matter of time.

Before Momma left the hospital that day I made arrangements for Homecare to come on the following Monday. The weekend is eternal when you are waiting. The days and nights are endless cycles of more waiting. Minutes melt into hours as you wait. Homecare arrived about 10:30a.m. and immediately determined Momma's condition had worsened over the weekend. She must see the doctor. That meant transporting her from point A to point B, not an easy task in her state. After seeing the doctor, through some grace of God, he made some calls and was able to secure a room at The Finley Hospital in their Skilled Nursing Unit. It bought us some time while we waited to hear if she had been accepted at the nursing home we applied to. Title 19 is a process that evaluates whether you are eligible for residence in one of the state run facilities they operate. They want to know what funds you have, savings or stocks, insurance or bonds or rich Uncles. Red tape. But it's the only place available and so you settle.

The Skilled Nursing Unit in the hospital is for rehabilitation purpose, not for those who fall under the heading, "only a matter of time." They are good and caring people and they provide a peace of mind while you are waiting and preparing for approval to get into a home. When we were able to finally transfer Momma from Skilled Nursing to Sunnycrest Nursing Home, she was still aware and able to understand all that was happening. She accepted her fate without complaint. Under the circumstances, Momma didn't have an active role in the decisions being made; there was just no choice in the matter. A sad situation to be confronted with. It wasn't something she and Dad ever talked about or prepared for. Seems they didn't talk about a lot of things, not to each other, not to anyone. And so you settle, quickly.

Making advance preparations for the unforeseen should be something people think about upon entering adulthood. Like it or not, sometime in your life you are going to be faced with events that cause you to make uncomfortable decisions for those you love. I think being prepared takes a lot of the worry and stress out of it. I see advance preparations as a gift. It is hell if you have to do it, especially when there is no choice. Hell for you, hell for the one you must now decide for.

Momma never complained one little bit though she accepted the decision. I think she too was relieved. Knowing she was under the constant supervision of health professionals made the transition easier. But she knew, it was only a matter of time, it went without saying.

A flurry of paperwork followed once Momma got to the nursing home. Names and dates, who, what, when, where. Contacts and phone numbers. Living wills, as well as last wills and testaments needed to be made. Once completed we went to visit her in her new home, she had a semi-private room. Semi-private meant four beds, four privacy curtains, and one room. Shortly after she was settled in, a nurse came in to test Momma's mental well being. She asked Momma if she knew her own name, date of birth, who the president was and where and why she was here. The nurse had Momma repeat words and spell them, do mathematical problems and write. A very dignified process to determine her agility. Considering what Momma had been through in the last few days, I believe she performed quite well.

Momma was scared; you could see it in her eyes. Scared for her own self, scared for Dad, scared about her future. She would be alone in a strange setting to face those fears, to come to terms with the knowledge, "it was only a matter of time".

It must be a difficult thing to face death. We do not grasp its concept; only that it is an ending. Because we do not understand it, we fear it. It holds a mystery beyond our comprehension. We cannot control, dominate or manipulate it. Death fails to sway under our rule despite our continual search for immortality.

Watching the progression of death in someone you love is terrifying. It causes you to face the realization that you too will be making this same passage one day. You suddenly become aware how powerless human beings really are. We can ease the suffering, medicate the pain but cannot take away the inevitable.

For the next three weeks Momma seemed to level off under the professional care and kindness she received. Hope grew once more in those few short weeks but fate was not yet finished with Momma.

In the meantime I had returned to my home in Colorado and arranged for Momma to call on Christmas. I hustled to get appropriate gifts purchased, wrapped and sent in time for the holiday. I did not want Momma spending Christmas without gifts. It was hard enough knowing she was spending Christmas away from her own home without her thinking she was alone or forgotten. We talked for a long time on Christmas. As we talked, she knew; she knew I knew it was the beginning of the end. We cried when we said goodbye and we hung up not knowing for certain what the next days held in store or if there would be any more days.

She was ever on my mind and I waited for the phone to ring. Long sleepless nights filled with worry and thoughts and hope. The phone rang.

Momma had taken a turn for the worse and was back in the hospital bleeding internally. Things did not look good. I made arrangements again to go back home. The long sleepless nights in the process are forgotten when set against the balance of life and death. The journey taken is one for both the living and the dying. The experience changes you and each grows toward a directed path.

On the day I flew back, Momma had gotten released from the hospital and was back at the nursing home. When I arrived I walked into her room feeling numb. I was nervous and frightened. Another thousand miles and lack of sleep put me into a dazed and vulnerable state of mind. I didn't know what to expect from the next few days. As I entered her room, I immediately saw that Momma was no longer alert or able to stay awake. She talked between stages of consciousness, not fully present to the here or now. When she did awake to the moment, her gaze was distant and aloof. It appeared as if she was watching something indiscernible to human vision and she was attentive to whatever it was she was now seeing. She would apologize for her inability to stay focused and quickly slip back to wherever she had wandered off to; she was tired, tired and worn out.

She now slept almost twenty-four hours a day, refusing food and only sipping at water. The monster was winning. Friends drifted in and out, bringing cards and flowers and well wishes. I think, despite Momma's non-awake state, she knew they were there.

An occasional smile would cross her face before lapsing further into that place she now found comfort in. She no longer responded to the conversations going on around her, it was far beyond that; it was sonly a matter of time.

When you stand with a dying person as they advance toward death, you begin to grasp the idea more clearly that there is a life beyond this one. I watched for days as Momma tried to let go of the here and now and make her way into the then and there. I was intensely conscious of the struggle, the fluttering eyelids, the images only she could see, as well as the comments she made about what she was witnessing. I knew then and there she was communicating with a power, an influence, and a love more persuasive than any she had ever encountered in this life. Her frustration was apparent as she tried to physically and mentally rid herself of the restrictions this existence placed on her. As I stood watching Momma die, I realized the journey we make from this life to the next is inward, returning to that place inside us where the essence of who we really are stands waiting for our return. Experiencing death brings everyone to new places and the experience marks the memory like a hot branding iron. You will always remember those moments as you walk the path together.

I screamed and cried and cursed once I returned to the safety and solitude of my motel room. It took the better part of one night to get it all out of my system. The questions, the pleas, the inability to comprehend what was happening all surfaced at once. I spent hours that night in Momma's tender care, talking and crying and preparing. I knew she was there, I could feel her presence everywhere around me. Holding me as she did when I was a child, kissing away my tears and vanquishing the fears I had that brought us together now like this. That night, in the motel room, Momma and I mixed spirits and something deep inside me washed away the pain. It allowed us to say to each other the things we needed to say and to give each other the permission to let go.

The doctor suggested that Hospice be contacted. They made arrangements to provide support and nursing care that is specifically directed toward those patients and their families who are facing death. They met with us on the Friday before Momma died and we listened to the services they offered, as well as further assistance during times of need. Hospice is a wonderful organization. They give the caregivers, (family members), the opportunity to take a break. It gives you a chance to attend to things long pushed aside, put on hold during the last few weeks. They are close at hand when any need arises or to answer questions you may have. Of course there was more paperwork to go through and more questions to answer but well worth all involved. They gave us booklets and pamphlets to read concerning additional questions and concerns one might have during this time but best of all they are real people with compassion and genuine love of the work they do. Bless them all! The booklets provided, told of what to expect in the last days, hours and moments as your loved one takes their last steps in the journey of life. Taking it all in within less than a week was difficult and tiring. I tried to talk to Dad and have him read the material but he wasn't present to any of it. He was consumed by his love, by his fear, by his hope.

Momma and Dad's life together was not going to be conquered. Dad held on way past the end, hoping and praying for a miracle. A miracle that would give back to him what was slowly being stolen away. I could not tell him otherwise nor did I try too hard. Maybe it was easier for him when the time did come. Each of us deals with death differently and the sadness hasn't left his face even today. It defeated him. Now that the end was imminent, it became increasingly important to Dad how much Momma had eaten or if she had, how much liquid she had that day and if she was comfortable. He repeatedly asked her if she needed anything but most of all it was important that he tell her over and over, how much he loved her.

Hospice visited with Momma three times before she died. They increased pain medication to ease any physical hurt she might be having, as well as discontinue unnecessary care. Things like getting up in the chair at mealtime, going to the dining room or walking. Huh! If Momma had been up walking around when I got there, I'd have thought the Lord Jesus Christ Himself was her doctor! Hospice now monitored which pills Momma needed to take, her blood pressure, heart rate and oxygen level. They watched all her "vitals" to determine where she was on her journey home. Some things were no longer standard practice. Keeping the patient free from pain and comfortable becomes the order of importance. Hospice made that possible for Momma and I am grateful to them.

On Monday the week Momma died, I had to go back to Colorado. I needed to take care of some things that had been put on hold two weeks ago when I left. I also needed some time to be away and collect my thoughts. I had previously planned on going home that upcoming Friday prior to being summoned sooner. I had tickets already purchased and decided the two or three days in between would allow me to get things together. Being gone didn't really change anything though, I spent the entire time going over the inevitable, planning, preparing, going through clothes and picking out appropriate garments to take with me this time. I kept an emergency suitcase packed for the last two months, not knowing when I would be summoned to go at a moments notice. I used it twice during that time. Now I repacked and sorted through again, preparing to go home again one last time in a couple days. Momma had other plans. She always did do things her own way and this time was no different. Hospice called me on Wednesday morning to tell me "**IT**" was real close. They did not think she would live until Friday when I had originally planned on returning. I called immediately and changed my tickets, getting a flight leaving the following morning at 6:30a.m. The ride to the airport with my friend was long; we talked talk, knowing the next few days were going to be sad. We talked and prayed.

My flight left about 45 minutes late preventing me from making my connection in Minneapolis. I ended up with a four-hour lay over. More time to think. Think and wait and hope and pray and worry. Though I had said my goodbyes to Momma earlier that week, they didn't seem timely or real. I wanted one last moment with her, one last minute of love. Now sitting waiting, watching the clock tick, I knew each second was one less I would have with Momma. Like a time bomb clicking off the seconds to detonation. I finally got into town at 4:30p.m.

Stepping off the plane in my hometown, Dubuque, Iowa, is like stepping into the past. Returning there is like looking at an old photograph album. Everywhere you turn things are a constant reminder of the life you lived and the people you left behind. You see them now everywhere, at the mall, at the grocery store, at the cemetery.

I raced to the nursing home just as Dad was leaving. He wasn't surprised to see me even though I hadn't taken the time to call and tell him I would be there sooner than expected. He wasn't surprised at all; in fact I don't think he knew I was gone for the day and a half at all. His thinking wasn't clear or focused during those days. Together we went up to Momma's room, both hoping together now. But hoping for what? I didn't know but it seems like if you quit hoping, if you give up, you've quit loving. Momma wasn't really there that late afternoon when we went in. She was now at the far end of the tunnel they tell us we make our way through. The tunnel with the light at the end of it. She was knocking at the door where light and warmth and other people who have journeyed before you are waiting. People waiting to welcome you to your new life, helping to make the transformation easier from the here and now to…wherever.

I watched it on Momma's face. The expressions coming and going. She could see them, she recognized them. They were beckoning to her, calling to her. She twitched and groped not quite ready to go but still not wanting to remain here. They must have had to do a lot of convincing to get Momma to cross that threshold. Her knuckles were white around the bars of the hospital bed, not yet willing to release the hold she had on this life. I don't think Momma was scared any more, she didn't appear to be, but I was.

I stood along side that bed talking and watching Momma die for nearly two hours. Supper trays were being passed out in the hall beyond and every so often a staff member stopped in to see how things were going or if there was anything Momma needed. But there was nothing anyone here could offer that would be of help to her now. Momma was running, no longer taking her time. Running to get where she was going quickly and I watched. I just stood there watching my life giver, giving hers up.

"It's just a matter of time". What does that phrase mean when you are standing along side of someone you love who is dying? Just a matter of time. Today those words haunt me; they are so empty, so void of meaning. Those words contain no hope; they offer nothing to the dying and little to those left behind. Left behind now to deal with time. Time for what? All the time you had is over, now you have only time to wait. Precious few moments in time to watch all of time come to a halt. It gives you an eerie feeling to know this is what it is like to die. Standing watching Momma die, leaving me for good, alone to only memories. You are left trying to decipher the confusion of days and weeks and hours leading up to those last precious gasps of labored breath that signal the end. I talked to Momma in those last final moments as if nothing had changed. I talked to Momma in those last moments of our lives together just like we use to, sitting out back on the porch swing together, planting gardens, planning holidays and just having the freedom of time. Time that was slipping away from us both now in a heartbeat.

The last moments of someone's life are not for the faint of heart. It's an awakening to watch death creep in casting its shadow over the life of someone you love. The sights and sounds and even the smells shock you. At that moment your emotions are shot to hell. There is a certain feeling that permeates within the room of a dying person; it becomes sacred ground. The silence is overwhelming. No one talks or thinks beyond what is happening. You are just present to the moment and the situation now facing you. A situation you have no control over. You find yourself deep into those moments. Memories flood your thoughts. Little things that yesterday meant nothing now become some of the most important things in your life. Birthdays, Christmas, dressing up for Halloween, it all comes back clearly. Every detail and you vow to commit them to memory. Those who work with the dying are Godsends. I cannot imagine being in that role, knowing how to respond, what to say or not to say is a gift. I don't think it is something you could ever get used to. Each experience must leave some sort of mark upon your being that you carry with you forever.

In the last hour of Momma's life, she and I went over our lives together. It was comforting for me to recall for both of us what she no longer could. She would have liked it that way. The death of someone you love tears at your inner being. There is nothing at all you can do to shield or protect the one you love from what is happening, nothing at all. You are both in the hands of God.

Momma didn't seem to suffer when she finally took her last breath. There were no bells, whistles or last hurrahs, she just stopped breathing. Just like they said she would. It was no longer a matter of time; time had stopped for Momma.

Momma was officially pronounced dead at 8:00p.m, January 30th, 2003. The medical term for her cause of death is listed as Dilated Cardiomyopathy. In layman's terms that means her heart muscle had turned to mush, unable to pump the necessary life giving blood throughout her body. As a result of that it had been necessary for Momma to spend the last two years of her life on oxygen, breathing becoming more and more difficult until today.

Before Momma became ill she sported a walker that she decorated with a horn and a little stuffed toy. Regardless of her failing condition, she was always ready and willing to go off shopping or wherever you were willing to take her. You couldn't keep her down as long as you allowed her enough time in the afternoon to "recharge". That recharging included being able to watch "her story", Days of Our Lives. She was a diehard fan. She remembered the very first episode, the episode that got her hooked. Everyone knew better than to disturb Momma between 12:30p.m. and 1:30p.m. I'd give anything to sit and watch it today with her.

No matter how well you think you have prepared yourself, no matter what you may have read, death is still alarming. It is hard to stand there watching someone you love no longer breathe. You want to do something, anything to restore that to them. You want to scream for help, take hold of them until life returns. But you don't. You just stand there staring at the now lifeless form, watching the now fading signs of the battle waged, the battle lost. Watching Momma die was a revelation. Somehow I realized we would be together again. I didn't just believe it, I knew it. I could feel how close we were despite the veil between us. It created a feeling of peace within me as well as a sweet relief for Momma.

In the minutes after Momma died everything changed. When you walked into her room you'd listen. Listen for the raspy, gurgling breathing that now was quieted. The sound you had come to recognize was gone, silenced. There was nothing to hear but your own breathing against the still backdrop of death. I stood looking down on the bed where what remained of Momma lay. I couldn't cry. It didn't seem necessary for some reason.

My emotional state leaned more toward a calmed reprieve. I realized the form lying upon the bed was no longer my Momma; she belonged to someone else now. The days and weeks and months of waiting seemed to catch up with me at that moment and I was suddenly aware how exhausted I was. I felt weak, my life old and used. The events of the past days played like a movie in my mind. Our lives together permanently recorded in my memory.

Momma was always making excuses for the shortcomings in other people. Excuses she made up to cover up the hurt she felt. The most important thing in Momma's life was time. Time with her family, time with her friends. Excuses, excuses, excuses. I heard words like, I woulda, I shoulda, and I coulda from so many people wishing they had. I think grief, in many cases stems from guilt. Momma and I spent our time together enjoying who we were, comfortable and grateful for the minutes we had, knowing how quickly those moments slip away. We honestly enjoyed each others company and knew how precious the gift of time really was. Neither one of us carried any regrets about what we shoulda done, or coulda done, or woulda done together given more time. I felt good knowing it wasn't necessary to go through the process of wishing I had spent more time with her or come to see her more often or been more thoughtful. I am 48 years old, a mere blink in the passing of time. I know the time I did have with Momma on this earth, in our lifetime together, was quality time and my soul rejoices in that knowledge. I gave to Momma what she cherished most, time; and she in turn gave that to me. I think grief comes out of feelings of guilt and loss; the inability to recapture what is gone forever. An opportunity missed in the short span of time we have in this world. An opportunity missed to make a difference and to love. It's only a matter of time and in the end excuses don't mean a thing. Excuses hold no water and you can no longer hide behind them. Grief, regrets, guilt. Momma isn't here to make excuses for anyone, anymore.

Dad and I were in the room together shortly after Momma died. Dad had left briefly to get something to eat and while he was gone, Momma made her exit. I believe Momma knew it would have been too difficult for Dad to be there when she finally passed on and so chose to take the opportunity to save him further suffering. We spent the next 30 minutes with her remains while waiting for the funeral home to come and take her away.

Dad on one side of the bed, me on the other. We just stood there looking down at Momma, talking and waiting.

Dad had spent hours with Momma, sitting with her, holding her hand, talking to her, loving her. You could see their love that night as he stood hanging on one last minute. One last look at the woman he must now let go of and separate himself from forever. He just stood there looking and loving. Death is sad. There is a deep ache that comes from watching someone you love let go of the love of his or her life. Dad is truly only half of himself now, lost and alone.

Momma and Dad spent 56 years enveloped in their love. A love that saw them through the entire vow they made to each other and to God on January 16th, 1947. Through better or worse, 'til death do us part. They had only just celebrated an anniversary 14 days ago. They met right out of service, Dad was in the Navy and Momma was in the Coast Guard. They were inseparable since. They made a good life together, not without its ups and downs but one filled with respect, dedication and love. Today, Dad seems lost, Momma's death has taken away so much of his reason in life. I feel he is only going through the motions not fully alive as he once was.

Webster's Dictionary defines death as, "a permanent ending of all life in a person". It also defines dead as, "lacking positive qualities, such as warmth, vitality, interest, brightness and brilliance. Wholly indifferent. Without feeling, emotion or power." When death did finally make its uninvited appearance in our lives, it struck two-fold. It escaped, without recourse, taking Momma with it and left those of us remaining with a sense of deadness that enveloped our person. Death had accomplished what it had come to do.

At 9:00p.m. we left the nursing home, placing Momma in the hands of the director from Behr Funeral Home. That is difficult, entrusting someone now to take your Mother away and prepare her for viewing. Pretty her up so folk aren't shocked at what they see. Giving a last impression for others to remember her by. They miss out on the last impression, the last moment when Momma was still alive.

I feel I have been blessed and gifted to have had the chance to stand with Momma during those last weeks and final hours of her life. Gifted because I was able to be with her as she made the journey closer to the final stage of life and blessed by what I witnessed in her passing. Much of my life has changed, not only because she is no longer a living presence in my life but also because her death made me understand so much about living. Momma's death has shown me we are never without hope. I believe this was her final gift to me, a story of love, a story of hope, when hope seems so far out of reach. Each of us comes to hear their own music, their own song, in their own time. The rhythm that the universe creates for each of us individually. The song becomes a spiritual encounter, not in the religious sense but as energy, a force that animates the being. I am not a religious person, I do not profess to a structured creed or faith but standing with Momma caused something, some doorway to be jarred open inside me and even if I tried, it cannot be closed. I have attempted to ignore it, to quiet it, to close my ears to its sound but it will not be silenced. It is that still small voice which must be heard.

I cannot make this point clearer; you will never see the one you love again in this life. You cannot recapture lost moments. You have but one Mother and if you choose not to be a part of the last hours or seconds of that life, you will carry that loss with you the rest of your life. Apologies, remorse and guilt will not take that away. Standing, being, loving in those last moments is the final gift you can ever give.

Dad took care of notifying some of the close relatives, I would complete the rest of the list in the morning. It had been a long day and I could not fathom the idea of repeating the ordeal several times to various people. I returned to my room at the motel to pass the night knowing time was no longer a matter to Momma. I contacted my two friends who were waiting to hear from me. We talked for a while about the upcoming days; their support was a comfort to me now. They both had been through the same thing with their parents and that eased much of my concerns. Arrangements had already been made for them to fly in the following day to help with many of the tasks now facing us. They both knew Momma very well and became a part of the extended family. I was looking forward to their assistance and support in the coming days. I spent the remainder of the night in a wake/sleep state. Thoughts and dreams intermixed to the point where I wasn't able to identify one from the other. I remember one part of the long night though and that was when I lay there half here, half somewhere else. I felt Momma touch my shoulder and say my name. I felt it. I'll never forget it. She wasn't sick anymore or helpless. She was young and whole. I remained awake the rest of the night just holding on to that memory.

The days that follow the death of someone you love are painful, painful and sad.

Where only days ago you spent time waiting, now you have hundreds of things to think about and take care of. All the time you once had is now rushed to get things completed and finalized. Arrangements for the funeral must be made and the realization of the last few days begins to hit home. You do not have the opportunity to practice, it is a time you must be at your best in the worst possible scenario. You find things out about funerals that you don't want to know. It is a time to make decisions about how you want your loved one presented and preserved. Clothes must be picked out for the mortician to dress the body in, caskets and vaults, prayers as well as the obituary must be thought about and decided upon. Dad and Momma had gone to the funeral home years ago to pick out the necessary items essential for death. When we got there the funeral director, Kathy Behr, had Momma's "wish list' waiting for us to look at. She explained all the articles and fundamental items necessary and the ones that Momma had chosen. But that was years ago when death seemed so very far away, back when both Momma and Dad were healthy and any real thoughts of dying were the farthest thing from anyone's mind. Today it was fact; it was real and had to be dealt with regardless of how we felt. Nothing had been "cast in stone" nor had anything been prepaid for. Nothing had been set aside to cover the cost and the life insurance Dad had for Momma was fitting for the 1960's, not 2003. Funerals add up fast and every thing you make a decision upon or want has a price tag on it. Both Dad and Momma were on a fixed income and there was little if any extra money to rely on. We went down to the showroom where caskets are on display. We took a tour looking at all the coffins available to send your loved one home in. The one Momma had picked out was a metallic rosy pink one, with matching satin padding and pillow. I picked the lovely brown wooden pine one, about $1200.00 less. I am practical and know in my heart the paraphernalia set before you is for your own peace of mind, not your loved ones'. It is not a good time to make decisions like this; your mental state is weak, confused and inattentive. It is a great opportunity to spend a lot more money than you have. There are about 6 different vaults to choose from, each a little more expensive than the last. Each one does the same thing; each one is approved by the State. Vaults are necessary to prevent the ground around the casket from collapsing and washing away. I chose the first one. I do not think the decisions I made concerning the casket and vault were lacking in love. I think if Momma had had to make the decision for me, she too would have chosen the same ones for me. I do not believe Momma felt slighted in the least bit.

Momma and I would occasionally talk about what we would like when we die, usually just passing thoughts. The only thing Momma was strictly adamant about was to see to it she had a full Military burial. She was entitled to it, she had earned it.

Seven rifles fired three times on the day Momma was buried, sending her off with the salute she deserved. The buglers played taps and her casket bore the stars and stripes, or "colors" in Military terms. She had served her country and now her country was sending her home. It's a chilling experience. The bugles moaned and wailed, first one and then off in the distance another echoed, calling to Momma. It goes right through you, right through your being, piercing your heart, piercing your soul. The American Legion gives you those empty shotgun shells as a memorial and also presents you with her flag. You shake a lot after that, you're not the same.

The whole while you are standing watching someone die, you realize you are as helpless as they are. You are totally reliant on others for answers as well as the next steps you need to take. When the wait is finally over though, you are alone and left to your own resources. You are empty and emotionally drained. All the time you had before is now gone and you find you must fight your way through three or four frenzied days of uncertainty and rushed decision making. There is no rehearsal, no chance to work the bugs out. Your performance relies on your ability to act out an unpracticed scene on the stage of life.

I found that many people who come to "pay their respects", expect certain things from the family members. Several times during the two days, people would look at me with pity, enquiring how I was holding up, only to be surprised by my composure. I tried to explain that though sad, I was at peace with it all. I did not have any regrets and I knew Momma and I would be together again. Some people don't want to hear that. I think it scares them. I will miss Momma terribly. I already was missing her but my sadness was not so much in her death but in my own inability now to call her or visit with her. Sadness on the inability to share those moments only she and I were able of sharing. I am not a tower of strength, not by any means and I never stopped feeling the love we shared. I would give anything to return to a time when my pains were kissed away and I knew nothing about death and loss. I will miss Momma every time I hear certain songs, songs that she and I sang together. We had many favorites but the one that stood out the most was "Always" I guess you could say it was our song. It said it all. "I'll be loving you Always, not for just an hour, not for just a day, not for just a year, but Always". I will miss Momma late at night and early in the morning. I will miss Momma when I can't call her to tell her important news or no news at all but just to know she is there. I will miss her every minute of every day.

I think each person enters their own personal world with a loved one when they die. A place where their souls can meet to say goodbye, one on one. I cannot share the emotions or pain I felt, anymore than others can share theirs. Death is a personal thing, to personal for words. I can have compassion and empathy with another but cannot totally get into others pain and suffering, nor others into mine. It is so personal, that you and your loved one are the only ones that can enter that place together. I believe by entering into that place of pain, it allows us to come directly in contact with who we are, where we can speak openly and honestly with the person passing on. It is as close to our own death as we will ever experience in this life without actually crossing the line. It is a night of darkness and void going on in our inner beings that reveals to us the mystery and sacredness of all life. Words fail us in these moments. Language lacks the means to express the hurt. I believe it was planned like that, felt not spoken. You will ever be present to the moment.

Momma's death showed me regardless of what life holds for us we are never without hope. It was her final gift to me. She allowed me to see, to come to know life does not end with death but rather we are released unto ourselves. Freed from the restraints this life has on us. When someone you love dies you are changed. That which you once took for granted is no longer here. I long to pick up the phone and call Momma. I want to talk to her about everything or nothing at all, just to hear her voice.

When I think about Momma now I can better understand the concept of God.

Unconditional love. Through Momma's love I discovered who I am. She allowed me to learn and grow from my mistakes, all the while giving me wings to fly. She let me go out and make a mess of things, and then welcomed me back with open arms and heart. She offered advice, at times to ears that refused to hear and turned a blind eye at my failings I am sure she knew would occur. Momma's death and her undying love have brought me even further in my belief and understanding of God, in life, love and hope. The whole process was and is an awakening and a walk toward a new life for both Momma and me.

January in the Midwest can be one of two things weather wise, cold or colder. The temperature fell well below zero most nights and the daytime temperatures were a balmy 10-15 degrees. I was frozen. Coming from Colorado where we had been having 70 degree temperatures did little if anything to raise my spirits.

We met at the funeral home at 2:00p.m. the day of Momma's wake service. It was a Sunday and the service was to be held from 3:00p.m. until 8:00p.m. that evening. It is traditional for the family members to meet and view the remains prior to the start of the public service. Any changes that need to be made can take place at that time. It also gives the family a few quiet moments alone or together to prepare for the upcoming five hours. The wake service took place in an old Victorian Mansion that years and years ago came to be a Behr Funeral Parlour. It is a stately old structure and was a perfect setting. We had all been inside the building before; it was sort of a family choice. I suppose once you need a funeral parlour you stick with the chosen one whenever the need arises. Dad and Momma had been friends with the original funeral directors, Norb and Mary Behr, for years and when it became necessary for them to use their own services, their daughter, Kathy, carried on the tradition. It really was all in the family.

Momma did not look much like she had. Death has a funny way of changing your appearance. I really don't think many people, except Dad and I noticed the change. The pain and suffering was wiped off Momma's face, replaced now with a look of peaceful contentment, not at all the last impression left upon my mind just two days ago. I could not get over how much Momma resembled Estelle Getty. Even a couple of friends I mentioned this to were in agreement with me. Momma never resembled any one but herself while living and I now thought this so very odd. It confirmed my thoughts and feelings that the body lying there in the coffin was no longer my Momma. I imagine she was in attendance though, waiting excitedly to see some of her old friends again and dwell among the relatives. Listening to the latest gossip and catching up on news. Momma would have enjoyed herself. It seems like the one time when everyone willingly gets together, sort of a reunion. When it's over everyone goes back to his or her life again, touched in some way by the experience, by the loss. Death stays with you for a while. Little by little over time the wounds heal, but the scars remain to remind us of how fragile life really is and how quickly the flame is snuffed out.

Wake services are a test of endurance, to see how much you really can tolerate. It is not enough to have clung to the last threads of life with someone you love; now it is necessary for you to live it over and over and over with a multitude of people. Scores of folk came to see Momma one last time and to express their sympathies. Flowers and cards and memorials rolled in as tokens of love. Momma would have been impressed.

She would have cried to know how many people and their lives she had touched during the years she lived on this earth. Even weeks after, Dad was still receiving notes and cards from people who had only just heard. What a grand exit Momma made!

The day before the wake service I made a picture board. I placed it at the entrance of the funeral home for people to take a look at Momma's brief time here on earth. I poured over photographs, searching for highlights that would tell the story of who this woman was. I was fortunate to be able to do that, it gave a real feeling to those who did not know her like I did. It showed others the many facets of her personality and life. The spirit that will always be with us.

For two full hours there was a steady stream of well wishers and acquaintances. Each time I had the chance to look up, the room was flooded with people. When at last the crowd thinned it gave us all the opportunity to share some stories, some memories with each other. I think that is an act of love, to share with each other who and how Momma will be remembered. Little things that stand out in each individual life. There were tears; there were silent moments when words could not be spoken. It was at that time Momma had her arm around all of us, holding us in her heart through memories shared.

By the time the first day had ended there was nothing to do but go and prepare for the next. It is a numbing experience and exhausting to the mind and spirit. You drag yourself through those moments, suddenly aware how strong you really are. You carry an almost impossible weight upon your shoulders, the weight of years and love and memories.

In 1977 I wrote a poem. I was growing up and into that sort of thing at the time. Back when it was "cool" to write poetry. Most teenagers and young adults were expressing themselves by those means, who they were, how they felt, all looking for the meaning of life. I was no different. This is my poem.

The Vigil

> A lonely Mother sits praying
> By a glowing candlelight,
> Her wish is for her children
> Away this Christmas night.
> Her work worn hands are folded
> A tear forms in her eye,
> She reads her tattered bible
> As the many years fly by.
> No one has come to visit her
> Upon this blessed day,
> They say they're much too busy
> To be bothered in this way.
> A lonely Mother sits silent
> By a glowing candlelight,
> Her soul has gone to heaven
> She's gone home this Christmas night.

I am not a poet but I hold so close to me that poem because there is so much truth in it. Momma really liked it too and said it cut to the chase. Christmas time was special to Momma, she loved it. She enjoyed giving and really loved getting gifts.

In September before Momma died, she came out to Colorado to visit me. Because of her need for an oxygen tank, we decided to drive both ways. It is a long drive and it was necessary for us to make the trip, one way, in two days. On our trip back, we stopped in Council Bluffs, Iowa, for the night, staying at the Ameristar Resort and Casino. Momma had played a slot machine only once or twice in her life, never considering herself very lucky when it came to any risk taking ventures. For something different though I thought she'd enjoy tossing a few quarters into one of the machines. She played for about fifteen minutes or however long $20.00 takes, getting a spit or two. On one of her last pulls she hit a jackpot. $375.00. It was the most money Momma ever had of her own at one time in her life. She was thrilled. She got her picture taken and had the biggest grin on her face as they counted out the money to her. She made me promise not to tell anyone, she had already formulated plans for the cash. She spent every cent of that money on Christmas gifts for people because she could. While she was with me on that visit, I tried to think of things within her ability that would be fun and interesting for her, but never could I have planned on her winning at that slot machine. Thanks God!

You don't have the same amount of people thronging to a funeral mass as you do at the wake service. It is a closer knit grouping of people who come to send you off according to your religion. It is a ceremony and rite of passage after which those same close-knit people gather to break bread together. It is a solemn event and there are many tears. It signals the end. Up to now you just go through the motions, shaking hands, talking, hugging but this is it. The fat lady is singing. The reality of the whole thing is staring you right in the face. Once the casket is closed and goes to the church it is over. The pall is placed over the coffin and the service begins. There are no more looks, no more touches and no more goodbyes. Your loved one is in route to the eternal.

When I met with the priest, Father Barta, the Saturday before the funeral, we picked out readings and a couple songs for the service. Songs and readings that suited who Momma had been. When you listened to them you could relate the words to Momma's life. The priest was kind and made a few suggestions for the readings that made reference to women. During the liturgy, Father told the congregation of Momma's life and how she was the backbone of the family and the encouragement she afforded everyone who knew her. Momma was baptized and grew up Methodist, converting to Catholicism before marrying Dad. Because of her upbringing one prayer stood out to Momma and that was the 23rd Psalm. I made certain that it was part of the service. She knew it by heart and taught it to me as a youngster. Powerful words, words that Momma lived by and trusted.

Momma was born in 1922; those were tough years for everyone. Her family didn't have much; in fact one could say they were dirt poor. But through it all Momma brought much to her family and friends, along with strength and determination. She quit school to help finance some of the needs in her family. Her own father dying as a result of mustard gas poisoning during World War 1. She was sixteen and there wasn't much if any money available to care for the five other kids at home plus her mother. So she did what she had to do, she went to work to help support them. Ironically, her first job was at the very nursing home she died in. At the time she was employed though the facility was a TB Sanitarium. Momma was the first woman in Dubuque, Iowa, to enlist and enter the Coast Guard. She did so as a memorial to her own father. About two years before

Momma died the government issued Momma an honorary high school diploma. Since she quit school to help her family and serve her country, the government felt it was their duty to acknowledge the men and women who sacrificed so much for their country. Momma was so proud of that diploma and showed it off to just about everybody she knew. Momma unselfishly gave her entire life, in all she did and who she was. Momma had a dream, a vision. She met challenges with grit and fortitude, passing that on. In many ways I think to myself I have become my mother and I am proud of that thought. What better standards and principles to live by. I don't think if given the opportunity there was much Momma could not have accomplished but she chose instead to be a devoted wife and loving mother. Momma loved to watch the Rockettes perform. She could dance and do that thing they do with their legs pretty good but being 4'11" it was an ambition she never pursued. Instead, she and Dad would fend off those thoughts and go cut up some rug dancing. She loved to dance even in her wheelchair. Momma was no stick in the mud; she knew how to have fun and loved life. Momma really liked to get all gussied up, from head to foot. She was never completely dressed unless she had a hat on. A hat, matching gloves, shoes and "pocketbook". Dressed to kill. It was only fitting then, that as a send off, in Momma's honor, I wore not only a *"SKIRT"*, but also hat, gloves and shoes that matched. She would have been so proud. She would have beamed and said, "Hubba, hubba, don't you look classy!"

We marched out of St. Mary's Church with heads bowed along side Momma, ready to take the long ride to Linwood Cemetery. I do not know how funeral processions are performed in other towns but in Dubuque, Iowa, the procession has the right of way. You do not have to stop for red lights; you are the guest of honor.

We were the first to arrive at the graveyard and after the American Legion gave their ceremony we entered the chapel. This is the big send off. You have your choice, either in the chapel or at the graveside. I do not believe any one of us could have managed the graveside service. To me it was unthinkable and I am proud of those people who are capable of enduring that particular ceremony. Last prayers and thoughts are offered at this time and then it's all over. You pull yourself out knowing it is finished. All the hours and minutes spent throughout her life are left right there. If you dwell on that for too long I think it could have serious mental effects. The thought of burying someone is hard to allow into your mind. I profess a faith not to any structured religion, believing we are all a part of the whole and I wildly enjoy the natural world. I love to "play in the dirt" and I know we are like the seasons. In order to grow, we must die from this life to be reborn anew. I know this. I believe this. I understand all of this in the logical part of my mind, as well as the spiritual section but the portion of my mind controlled by my heart isn't as willing. The thought of putting someone you love into a hole and covering it with six feet of dirt is an image too horrifying to imagine. It is best not to allow your heart to control your thoughts at that time.

Those present for Momma's final send off gathered together to say their goodbyes and share a meal. For me eating was not something I felt like doing. In the last few days I had had enough goodbyes to sink a ship, I needed some hellos for a change of menu.

The days and weeks and months of watching and waiting and hoping were winding to a close. It was time to take another look at life. Another look at the lives that Momma left behind.

When all the hoopla was complete and the ceremonies were over, I returned to Momma's home. Her real home, where she and Dad had spent the last eight years of their lives together. Prior to that they lived in a house that got too big for them to handle and I moved them into Windsor Park, an apartment complex, that had been Xavier Hospital. It had been remodeled and had an elevator, restaurant, beauty salon, laundry and it's own chapel. It was perfect for mature citizens and they both came to enjoy their new lives there. Of course Momma missed not having her own yard but was grateful not to have to negotiate the stairs or worry about the upkeep of a six-room house anymore. She took on the task of Activity Director in her new home, throwing parties, having potlucks, welcoming new residents and providing all residents with something to look forward to. She would enlist the help of who ever was available and made sure everyone in house received birthday greetings, Christmas cards or get-well wishes as warranted. She neglected no one, that's the way Momma was.

I gathered together some of Momma's personal affects, things I wanted to keep and shipped them back to Colorado. In the days that followed, we sorted through clothes and hats and shoes, donating them to charities or organizations we felt could best use them. We responded to the cards and memorials left behind as expressions of love and did all the necessary elements of picking up the last pieces of a life now complete. It was over. Momma had moved. She was now in the best care available. She didn't have to worry about the pain she endured for so many years. She didn't have to be fearful of what the future held in store. She was at peace.

It was now a matter of proceeding forward, knowing that Momma may not be with us physically but that she hasn't really left us at all. She would continue to be my strength and courage in everything I did. She would live, everyday in my heart and in my soul. Just as present today, a thousand miles away as she was when her heart still beat. Encouraging me, crying with me and supporting me as she had done during our brief time together in this world.

I see Momma today as the tulips in the yard are blooming or watching the snow fall in the mountains. I have reminders of Momma everywhere I go and in everything I do. I know there are going to forever be little surprises in my life around every corner that pop up. Pop up and say, "Hi kiddo, I love you always, Momma". If it hadn't been for Momma and her love I wouldn't be who I am today, her light shines brightly within my soul, even on those cold, dark, lonesome days, reminding me she is always there. Thank you Momma, for being who you were, who you are and who you have become.

I love you Momma!

0-595-32615-3

Milton Keynes UK
Ingram Content Group UK Ltd.
UKHW020708211124
3012UKWH00013B/59